From Early American Paintbrushes

Colony to New Nation

Detail from THE MOUNTAIN FORD *by Thomas Cole*

ART TELLS A STORY SERIES

From Early American Paintbrushes

Colony to New Nation

BY CARELLA ALDEN

Based on the production From Yankee Paintbrushes, *presented in the Art Entertainments series for young people, at The Metropolitan Museum of Art*

PARENTS' MAGAZINE PRESS · NEW YORK

To Roberta

CONTENTS

CHAPTER ONE

AMERICA'S FIRST ARTISTS

When the Pilgrims landed at Plymouth in 1620, they were not just a band of people seeking freedom of religion. They were, in a sense, America's first artists, for each was a master craftsman of his trade.

There were skilled carpenters, brick-makers, and stone

Courtesy of Plimoth Plantation

A view of houses at Plymouth as they may have looked in the 1620s. Archaeologists found some of the early foundations of the original "Plimoth." From a study of early records, the settlement has been rebuilt.

Courtesy Ginsburg & Levy, Inc.

A sampler is a kind of test of a young girl, to show how many embroidery stitches she has learned, and how well she can do them. This sampler has a variety of stitches, including cross-stitch and even lace work.

cutters. "Shipwrights" could build and repair ships, "joiners" could join together wood for houses, furniture, doors, and cabinets. "Smiths" could forge cooking pots or farming tools from iron. "Gun-founders" could cast metals into muskets, and "tanners" could turn raw animal hides into fine leather.

Women were experts at weaving cloth, quilting, and embroidering. From the plants and herbs they grew in their gardens they made the colors to dye their cloth and thread. These things they taught their daughters. By age eleven, a girl could proudly show her mother a fine sampler she had made.

Courtesy, Essex Institute, Salem, Mass.

The Whipple House in Ipswich, Mass. was begun in 1638. Compared to a Pilgrim house it is very grand indeed, and shows us what a permanent New England home was like.

It was largely the skills of these Pilgrims, who had separated from the Church of England, that enabled them to form the first permanent English colony in New England.

As more and more people arrived, new places were selected for settlements. Trees were cut down for timber to build the houses, churches, and shops that became villages. Indian trails often became roads that connected the villages; then the villages grew into towns.

During this early Colonial period there were very few paintings, but there were art and decoration. Joiners made furniture of oak in strong, straight lines; then they decorated them with deep carving. Each design showed the originality of its maker, for he often made his own patterns.

Many parlors of New England houses looked like this one from the Thomas Hart House at Ipswich. The ceilings are low, which made the room easier to heat. The beams are exposed. The main feature of the room is the large fireplace which was used for heating, cooking, and lighting.

A cupboard

The Metropolitan Museum of Art
Gift of Mrs. Robert W. de Forest, 1933

Blacksmiths forged iron into works of art—perhaps an Indian archer. And stone cutters showed their talent as sculptors on gravestones.

The earliest houses were not painted, but painters painted the coaches people traveled in, the ships shipwrights built, even toys carved by gifted hands. And if the painter himself was gifted, he painted pictures on signs.

Signs were as commonplace to early Americans as

Photograph by Roberta Paine

Toy

*Detail from an engraving
by William Hogarth*

traffic signs are to us today. They hung in front of every store, inn, shop, and tavern. For those who could read, the pictures on the signs were pure decoration. For those who could not, the pictures told the people, particularly newcomers or travelers, what goods or services were available within.

As time passed, sign painters became quite competitive. The pictures got better, and the work of the painters was admired. When a new sign was hung out, people hurried up the street to view it. These signs made a kind of outdoor museum—America's first picture museum.

By the 1670s, some painters advertised on their signs that they would paint faces. These painters, and the grownups they painted, had probably never seen any pictures done by the great painters of Europe. When the

Colonial Williamsburg, Williamsburg, Virginia

The sign that hangs outside the Raleigh Tavern at Colonial Williamsburg in Virginia names the Tavern, and honors Sir Walter Raleigh, the Englishman who financed the first settlers in America on Roanoke Island.

Worcester Art Museum,
Gift of Mr. and Mrs. Albert W. Rice

A portrait of Mrs. Elizabeth Freake and her baby,
Mary, painted about 1674 by an unknown artist.

pictures were finished, both painter and sitter—the person
who was painted—were no doubt proud of them.

The pictures look flat because the painters lacked
proper training in drawing. The faces have little expression.
The figures look very stiff; more like dolls. In those days,
children dressed like grownups, so their best clothes were
very fancy. Painters seem to have spent more time painting

what their subjects wore than what they looked like. Still, these pictures are good examples of the earliest portrait painting in New England, and are very rare.

The story of pictures in New Amsterdam, later New York, is different. New Amsterdam was settled by the Dutch. The Dutch settlers loved pictures; they came from a country that prides itself on its great painters. Rembrandt was famous all over Europe for his portraits. Pieter de Hooch was capturing the feeling and the look of Dutch homes in Holland.

Museum of the City of New York

In this view of a model of New Amsterdam, we can see the big house of Governor Peter Stuyvesant at the lower left. Beyond it is the Fort with a flag flying, and a windmill. The wide road leading north through the town is Broadway. This famous New York City street was first laid out and named by the Dutch. To the right is a canal.

The Metropolitan Museum of Art,
Gift of Archer M. Huntington, in memory
of his father, Collis Potter Huntington, 1926

FLORA, oil painting by Rembrandt (1606-1669)

THE PANTRY, oil painting by Pieter de Hooch (1629-1683).
A Dutch home of the 17th century, with beamed ceilings and
fine tiled floors. Find a portrait that hangs on a wall.

Courtesy of The New-York Historical Society, New York City

Governor Peter Stuyvesant, by an unknown artist.

A portrait of Peter Stuyvesant, the Governor of New Amsterdam, was certainly not done by a sign painter, so a few fairly good painters must have come to the New World seeking adventure. But the painters who came to the New World were not the great ones. The great painters in Europe had no desire to go to a vast wilderness inhabited only by Indians and a scattering of colonists. What was there to paint? It would be left to native-born painters to paint America and Americans.

CHAPTER TWO

THE EARLY PAINTERS

From New Hampshire to South Carolina, the colonies grew. Wealth increased, from shipping, fishing, and the raising of tobacco and cotton. Ships, built in the colonies, sailed to England and Europe with colonial products, especially tobacco, that brought high prices. They returned with products the colonies needed, such as tools for farming and building. And from Newport, Rhode

The Metropolitan Museum of Art,
Gift of Col. and Mrs. Edgar William Garbisch, 1963

A plantation in the South. In the center is the Great House of the owner, which looks out over a river. Near the river is a warehouse where the produce from the land, such as tobacco and cotton, was stored. Some of the small houses in the scene were the homes of slaves.

Island to Charleston and down to the island of Jamaica, the slave ships arrived, bearing their human cargo from black Africa.

Pennsylvania, founded by William Penn, a Quaker, was the most liberal of the thirteen colonies. Through Penn's leadership, Pennsylvania welcomed all immigrants and offered religious freedom to all. There was friendship between the native tribes and the settlers.

The largest and most fashionable city in eighteenth-century Colonial America was Philadelphia. It was the

Courtesy of the Pennsylvania Academy of the Fine Arts
Joseph & Sarah Harrison Collection

PENN'S TREATY WITH THE INDIANS by Benjamin West

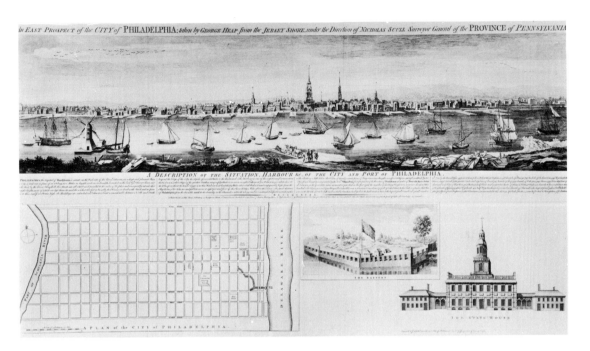

View of Philadelphia, before 1754

center for men of law, science, and literature. It was also
the port of entry for people arriving from the Old World:
from England, Scotland, Ireland, France, Sweden, and
Germany. Most were quite poor and came to escape
injustices in their native lands; but some were rich and
educated.

The Metropolitan Museum of Art

This is an 18th-century parlor with fine furnishings that belonged to Mr. and Mrs. Samuel Verplanck of New York City.

During the 1700s, fine new homes were built in all the colonies. The homes were furnished in the latest English fashion. Square, heavy-looking furniture had been the style of the 1600s; now the style had changed in England. Colonial furniture makers, following the new styles, created beautiful pieces, but with a definite American character. The furniture was smaller, less formal, and on the walls of these new homes portraits hung. Here, as in

England, portrait painting was the most popular form of painting.

Most of the portraits were painted by artists who had migrated to America. Some had had formal training in art and were quite good. If the clothes of their colonial sitters seem to attract your attention more than their faces, chances are that the artist, before coming to the New

DEBORAH HALL by William Williams, 1766

World, had worked as a "drapery painter," an assistant to a master painter. A drapery painter painted the clothes of the sitter while the master artist painted the face and was known as a "face painter." If the drapery painter was skilled, one could tell if a lady's gown was made of satin, velvet, or homespun wool. The face painter concentrated on trying to achieve a likeness of his sitter. In the colonies, the drapery painter painted both clothes and faces, so usually the fabrics turned out to be more believable than the faces.

These pictures have patterns of curving lines, which create grace and lightness. The people are placed in very grand settings, with imaginary landscapes in the background. People liked them on the walls of their homes because the women looked pretty and the men looked distinguished.

None of these migrant artists were great masters of painting. They were just good craftsmen who, like so many other people, saw an opportunity in a new land where almost everything, including portrait painters, was still needed.

CHAPTER THREE

THE FIRST AMERICAN PAINTERS

Joseph Badger was born in Charlestown, Massachusetts in 1708. First he was a house and sign painter; then he began to paint portraits. When his grandson, James Badger, was three years old, Joseph painted his portrait. The child is holding a bird. From the way he is standing—

The Metropolitan Museum of Art,
Rogers Fund, 1929

the position of his feet, arms, and hands—he looks more like a grownup than a three-year-old. That is because the artist lacked training in drawing.

In 1738, about the time Badger began to paint portraits, a boy named Benjamin West was born in the country, a few miles from Philadelphia. His father was an innkeeper. Although Benjamin had brothers and sisters to play with, he spent most of his time playing with the friendly Indians who lived in the area. The most fun was watching them paint their faces. When he was about seven, the Indians taught him how to draw pictures and make paints from colored earths and clays. It is said his mother gave him homemade dyes to add variety to his pictures and that the hairs for his brushes came from the family cat!

There were no art schools in the colonies for a talented boy like Benjamin to attend, nor were there any museums or art galleries where he might go to look at good pictures. There were, however, some engravings, which were copies of paintings done by the great artists in Europe. Young West, in turn, copied many of the engravings. By the time he was fifteen, Benjamin West was receiving commissions for portraits from nearby wealthy landowners. At seventeen he left home to attend college in Philadelphia as a scholarship student. West's good looks, personality, and charm won him many friends among Philadelphia families and he was soon painting their portraits.

The Metropolitan Museum of Art,
Gift of Mrs. A. S. Sullivan, 1919

Engravings were very helpful to young artists in the colonies.
Well-drawn figures like this could easily serve as models to copy.
This picture is called "The Separation of the Elements."

The engravings by Italian artists, showing scenes from history, interested West far more than portraits and so he decided that somehow he must get to Italy. To earn more money, he moved to New York. There, one of his customers, recognizing his talent, offered him help by paying for his passage.

When Benjamin West went to Europe he was accompanied by Samuel Powel, a wealthy young friend who had just finished college. Powel was not a painter, but he liked art. Together, they wandered among the ruins of ancient Rome. Through Powel, West met many people who became helpful to him. West spent three years painting in Rome. Then he went to London, where he was welcomed by England's leading painter, Sir Joshua Reynolds. With such recognition, the young man who had

The Metropolitan Museum of Art,
Harris Brisbane Dick Fund, 1936

When Samuel Powel and Benjamin West visited Rome, this is the way the ancient temple, the Pantheon, looked from the side.

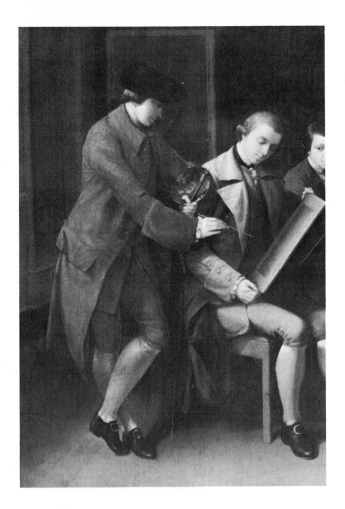

*Benjamin West and a student.
Detail from THE AMERICAN
SCHOOL by Matthew Pratt.*

received his first drawing lessons from Indians, decided
to remain in England.

News that Benjamin West had been so well received
soon reached hopeful young painters in the colonies.
Word that he had opened a school made them long to get
to London to study with him.

The first to go was Matthew Pratt, a friend of West's,
who was a portrait painter in Philadelphia.

The next to dash off was Charles Willson Peale. Born
in Annapolis, Maryland, he was apprenticed as a young

boy to a saddle maker. Later, he became a silversmith, and then a painter. Because of his talent as a painter, Maryland businessmen paid for his trip to London where he could study with Mr. West. Peale once said, "I would rather practice the use of my tools than ride in a coach drawn by six horses."

John Singleton Copley had been born in Boston, the year Benjamin West was born. When Copley was quite young, his father died and his mother married a man named Peter Pelham. Pelham was a portrait painter and an engraver, so young Copley grew up in an atmosphere of pictures and paints. From engravings he became familiar with the work done by the great painters of Europe, and from his stepfather he received painting lessons. He soon painted far better than his teacher. Like West, Copley, at seventeen, was painting portraits of prominent citizens. Because he had talent and worked hard, he became the most successful painter in Boston.

Courtesy, Museum of Fine Arts, Boston
Gift of Copley Amory

Copley painted this miniature portrait of himself on ivory.

Pencil drawing by Copley

He mastered the art of drawing, which gives a form to a picture. He had a fine sense for detail: a crisp white neck scarf, or a bright gold chain that kept a pet squirrel from scampering away. Such details enriched his pictures.

Copley had a talent for catching the likeness of a person and his personality as well. If you look closely at Copley's portraits you can almost hear his subjects speak and know what kind of people they were.

In 1766 Copley sent a portrait of his young stepbrother, Henry Pelham, to The Society of Artists in London. The picture received high praise from Sir Joshua Reynolds and

The Metropolitan Museum of Art,
Morris K. Jesup Fund, 1924

Copley painted this portrait of Mrs. Sylvanus Bourne in 1766. If you
compare this picture with the one of Mrs. Freake and Baby Mary (page 14),
you will see how much more life-like painting became in one hundred years.

The Metropolitan Museum of Art,
Gift of Bayard Verplanck, 1949

Daniel Verplanck sits on the front steps of his family's country home in
Fishkill, N.Y. Copley painted this picture in 1771, during a visit to New York.
The picture hangs in the parlor of the Verplanck house (page 22).

Benjamin West. Reynolds advised him to come to Europe to study. Copley was much encouraged by this, but had many orders to fulfill in Boston and New York and could not consider going to Europe at that time.

Three years later Copley married Susannah Clarke. She was the daughter of Richard Clarke, one of Boston's richest merchants. Because of his marriage, Copley now had friends among the very wealthy families of Boston, as well as the tradesmen and craftsmen with whom he had grown up. He was very popular with both.

Among his best friends was Boston's finest silversmith, Paul Revere. Copley painted Revere, not in his best clothes, but in his shirt and vest seated at his work bench. In the picture Copley showed the hands of an artisan, a skilled worker. They are strong hands, the kind needed for such metal work.

Not long after Copley painted this portrait, Revere put away his silversmith's tools. People were no longer buying silver, not even for investment, which had always been an important reason for its purchase. Times were fast changing. For Paul Revere, one of the most popular and energetic men in town, other matters became more important than making beautiful silver. These matters concerned the future of the colonies.

PAUL REVERE by John Singleton Copley

35

CHAPTER FOUR

THE ARTIST IN TROUBLED TIMES

England had gained new land in America from France. This included Canada and lands east of the Mississippi. A lot of money was needed for an army to defend the land and to govern the Indian population. To raise the money, England made her colonies pay heavy taxes. The colonies hated this. They had to pay taxes, but were not allowed any men in the English Parliament to represent them.

In 1765, a new tax, called the Stamp Act, requiring that all printed matter had to have a stamp on it, that had to be bought, made the colonists angrier than ever. They said they would not buy any English goods. The Stamp Act never went into effect.

The Metropolitan Museum of Art, Bequest of A. T. Clearwater, 1933

A Pine Tree shilling, the earliest type of colonial money. It was designed by John Hull, a Boston silversmith, and minted in 1652.

*In 1775, Paul Revere engraved copper
plates from which paper money
was printed. This note was valued at
24 shillings.*

   The Townshend Acts of 1767 placed an extra charge on
paper, glass, lead, painters' colors, and on tea!
   Colonial money lost much of its value and became
scarce. In Boston, people smuggled produce and goods in
and out of the city.

George III, King of England

The people in the colonies became divided. The Tories, or Loyalists, remained loyal to King George III, then king of England. Those who were against England's rule were known as Whigs. Often people did not know which side their own friends were on.

In Boston, troops were everywhere and mobs roamed the streets stealing and burning homes of people who were suspected of being Tories. Then one night violence broke out. A mob of citizens met up with some British soldiers in King Street near the Old State House. The mob shouted at the troops, trying to get them into a fight. Tempers ran high. A few people tried to break up the gathering, but without success. Suddenly, the mob surged toward the troops, and then a volley of shots rang out. Five men were killed. One of them was Crispus Attucks.

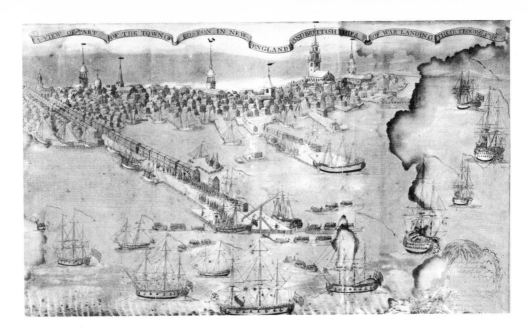

View of Boston in 1768. This was the city of Paul Revere and John Copley. Long wharves stretch out from the city into the harbor. On the wharves were the warehouses of the ship owners as well as the shops of merchants and craftsmen.

Esther Forbes, a famous historian, says about him: "He was well over six feet, was part Indian, part Negro, part white." Known as the Boston Massacre, the historic event was pictured by Paul Revere in an engraving.

BOSTON MASSACRE, by Paul Revere

In those days Paul Revere was much troubled. He told only a few friends what was on his mind. Revere had many friends among both the Tories and the Whigs. He also had friends among the British soldiers and officers. This was because he was always cheerful and thoughtful of others. But on certain nights he went to a tavern called The Green Dragon. Inside, he would climb a narrow flight of stairs that led to a small room. There he would meet with a mysterious group known as the Sons of Liberty. In quiet voices these men plotted how they might fight the injustices done to the colonies by England.

Paul Revere was a Son of Liberty. He became one of their couriers, or messengers. On horseback he carried messages to other Sons of Liberty, sometimes as far away as New York and Philadelphia. It was during these times that the leaders of the Sons of Liberty—such men as Joseph Warren, John Hancock, and Samuel Adams were having their portraits done by John Singleton Copley.

Courtesy of the American Antiquarian Society

The wrought-iron sign above the door, in the shape of a dragon, tells us this is The Green Dragon Tavern.

SAMUEL ADAMS by John Singleton Copley. Adams was the "elder statesman," the leader of politics in Boston at the time of the American Revolution. He was very good at leading discussions, and was a most important member of The Sons of Liberty.

Copley had continued to receive invitations from Benjamin West to come to London, but as he made a good living in the colonies, he thought it unwise to go. Still, a portrait painter in America was considered no better than any other craftsman. In England and other parts of Europe he knew painting was a more noble profession, with higher fees and possible royal commissions to make one famous. But even with work and study abroad, could he achieve such rewards? If he tried and failed and had to return to Boston, would it go against him and cause him to lose what he already had? These thoughts he argued back and forth in his mind. Finally, he made his decision.

In June, 1774, Copley sailed for England. Though in sympathy with the colonies, he was an artist who had to follow his dream. He did not see war ahead, for he left his family behind in Boston. Later on, when they had joined him in London, he wrote to his stepbrother, Henry, who by then was a young man, "Could anything be more fortunate than the time of my leaving Boston? Poor America. I hope for the best, but I fear the worst. Yet certain I am she will finally emerge from her present calamity and become a mighty empire. And the fine arts will one day shine with a luster not inferior to what they have done in Greece and Rome."

The Copley Family is a lovely, happy group. We see Mrs. Copley with John Jr., Mary, and Elizabeth. The youngest, a baby, sits on the lap of Richard Clarke. Mr. Copley stands to one side, paintbrushes in hand. He has painted his family and included himself.

CHAPTER FIVE

PATRIOTS AND PAINTERS

The night of April 18, 1775 was made famous nearly a hundred years later by the American poet Henry Wadsworth Longfellow. In his poem, Longfellow told how Paul Revere rowed across the river to Charlestown, watched for a signal from a lantern in the tower of Old North Church, then mounted his horse and rode "through every Middlesex village and farm," warning the people that the British were coming. The next afternoon, in Lexington, shots rang out across the village green. The Minute Men and British soldiers had fired on one another. The American Revolution had begun.

Lexington Historical Society, Inc.

The Minute Men of Lexington have been remembered in this sculpture, which stands on the grounds of the Buckman Tavern. It is very near the spot where Minute Men and British exchanged fire.

*MIDNIGHT RIDE OF PAUL REVERE is a 20th-century painting
by Grant Wood. He was inspired, not only by the known facts of
Revere's courage, but also by Longfellow's poem. Here we see the
dark silhouette of horse and rider galloping through a village.*

Illustration from Vuillier's
A History of Dancing, *1898*
Photo by Philip Evola

At that time, the Mayor of Philadelphia was the former traveling companion of Benjamin West, Samuel Powel. After four years of travel abroad he had returned home and purchased a splendid new house. In the ballroom, Philadelphia society danced the formal minuet. But in the parlors, such serious-minded men as Dr. Benjamin Franklin and John Adams met to talk of independence.

Powel's house was one of the most fashionable and elegantly decorated homes in America. A portrait of Mrs. Powel by Charles Willson Peale hangs over the fireplace.

DECLARATION OF INDEPENDENCE by John Trumbull clearly shows the face of each man who took part in this historic moment. The artist was an aide to General Washington and, later, a pupil of Benjamin West.

The Metropolitan Museum of Art,
Gift of William H. Huntington, 1883.

Miniature of George Washington, painted on ivory
by Charles Willson Peale.

The painter Charles Willson Peale, who had gone to
study with Mr. West in London, had returned. When war
broke out, he marched off as Lieutenant Peale, carrying
a musket with telescopic sights that he had invented, and
also a painting kit.

He fought under George Washington at the battles of
Trenton and Princeton, and, to help pass the bitter winter
at Valley Forge, Peale painted miniature portraits.

In the closing months of the Revolution, with the
Continental Army unpaid, short of supplies, and broken in
spirit, the British hoped to end the struggle with final
victories in the South. At that time George Washington

was at West Point in New York, and a French Major General, the twenty-four-year-old Lafayette, was in Richmond, Virginia commanding a large Continental force.

General Washington moved his army south and met up with Lafayette. The two armies marched to Yorktown, Virginia to challenge the British under Major General Cornwallis. The battle took only a few days. On October 19, 1781, Lord Cornwallis surrendered to General Washington.

The Metropolitan Museum of Art, Bequest of William H. Huntington, 1885

James Peale, a brother of Charles, painted this portrait of George Washington, which shows the victorious general after the Battle at Yorktown. The American banner flies high, while the British flags lay on the ground.

The Revolution was over. Americans could now get on with the business of building their new nation. Artists with their paintbrushes would be present to record it.

Philadelphia Museum of Art,
The George W. Elkins Collection

THE STAIRCASE GROUP
by Charles Willson Peale

CHAPTER SIX

A NEW MASTER PAINTER

When he was fourteen, Gilbert Stuart, who was born near Newport, Rhode Island, met a Scotsman who was visiting in Newport. When he learned that the Scot was a portrait painter, Stuart begged for lessons. He and his teacher, Cosmo Alexander, became close friends and, when Alexander returned to Edinburgh, Scotland, Stuart went with him. They were in Scotland only a short time when Alexander's sudden death forced Stuart to return home. He made a living for a while painting portraits, but Revolutionary war-time conditions made the purchase of portraits a luxury few could afford, so Stuart went to London.

In London, without money, half starved, and with no means of support, the twenty-two-year-old Stuart made his way to the studio of Benjamin West. West, who welcomed all artists, was especially happy to greet fellow countrymen, regardless of their talent. In Gilbert Stuart, however, he discovered a very fine talent.

Stuart studied under Benjamin West for five years. Like many of West's best students, he helped West by painting the drapery and background in his pictures.

Stuart exhibited portraits at the Royal Academy in London and they were all well received. Eventually he felt he had learned all he could from his master and so opened his own studio. He became more successful than he would have believed possible. But he had one special ambition: to paint the first President of the United States. He returned to America to do this and the picture became so popular that he had to make a number of copies.

In 1805, Stuart settled in Boston. By then there were many new painters in the United States, but now, for the first time, there was an experienced painter who could

The Metropolitan Museum of Art,
Rogers Fund, 1907

GEORGE WASHINGTON by Gilbert Stuart

advise them. Remembering the help he had received from Benjamin West, Stuart now helped many of these young painters when they visited him in his painting-room. He permitted some to watch him work. With others, he spent long hours discussing painting and explaining techniques. Each listened to advice, such as:

Good drawing is the most important of all; without it, coloring adds nothing.

Remember, the looking glass is one's best instructor. It should be used early in a painter's life so he gets to see his faults as well as his gifts.

The Metropolitan Museum of Art, Fletcher Fund, 1926

Stuart used his looking glass well when he did this portrait of himself.

JAMES MONROE, fifth President of the United States.
What did Stuart select as background and objects to show
that this man was a statesman?

As for coloring, sink your drapery and bring out the flesh. Flesh is like no other substance under heaven. It has all the gaiety of silk without its gaudiness and glare.

Create a background that points directly to the life of your sitter.

It is important, when composing your picture, to keep the figure in its circle of motion. While in London, I painted a picture of my friend Mr. Grant cutting a figure 8 on ice. I arranged his body to follow the circle of 8 motion, and I repeated the 8 in the background.

These were a few of the things that painters tried to achieve in their work. In America, Gilbert Stuart was the master of them all.

National Gallery of Art, Washington, D. C.,
Andrew Mellon Collection

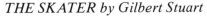

THE SKATER by Gilbert Stuart

CHAPTER SEVEN

AN ENDING AND A BEGINNING

The War of 1812, begun over "Free trade and sailor's rights," was mostly a naval war, and the pride of the United States Navy was the *U.S.S. Constitution.* She was nicknamed "Old Ironsides" because her beams of live oak and red cedar were so strong that British cannonballs

The Metropolitan Museum of Art,
Gift of Edgar William and Bernice Chrysler Garbisch, 1962

U.S.S. CONSTITUTION by Thomas Birch

bounced off her as though she were made of iron. When she first put to sea, Paul Revere watched from Boston Harbor with great pride. All the hardware and copper sheathing that covered the bottom of the powerful ship had been made by him.

Revere had become one of America's first industrialists, and it was during the War of 1812 that Revere's son asked Gilbert Stuart to paint portraits of his father and mother.

Courtesy, The Museum of Fine Arts, Boston
Gift of Joseph W., William B.,
and Edward H.R. Revere

PAUL REVERE
by Gilbert Stuart

Courtesy, The Museum of Fine Arts, Boston
Gift of Joseph W., William B.,
and Edward H.R. Revere

MRS. REVERE
by Gilbert Stuart

When the war was over, the borders between the United States and Canada were established, and the great sprawling land between the Mississippi River and the Rocky Mountains, bought earlier through the Louisiana Purchase, was open for settlement.

The flag about which Francis Scott Key had written the *Star Spangled Banner,* as he watched the bombardment of Fort McHenry at Baltimore, bore fifteen stars. More stars would soon be added as new states became part of the fast-growing nation.

The Hambleton Collection, The Peale Museum, Baltimore

As friendly relations were restored with Great Britain, many young painters dashed off to London with introductions to Mr. West from Mr. Stuart.

Neither West nor Copley ever returned to America. Copley's dream had come true. He was one of England's most famous painters, and he did paint for the King. (See page 60.)

For over fifty years, Benjamin West's studio was a gathering place for painters from Europe and America. Matthew Pratt painted that famous studio and called it "The American School." (See page 61.) West helped to found England's Royal Academy of Arts and, for a number of years, served as its President. He is called the Father of American Painting.

But the long popularity of portrait painting was drawing to a close. Soon artists in Europe and America would be leaving their studios to paint out-of-doors. And American painters would discover at last that there was far more to paint in their own land than in the old world of Europe.

In the Catskill Mountains, they would paint the colors and beauty of nature. They would picture scenes of daily life on the farms or along the rivers, and would show the native Indian and the buffalo. Finally, like the pioneers, they would reach the grandeur of the Far West and the Pacific Ocean. And, with their paintbrushes, they would continue to record the story of their country.

THE THREE YOUNGEST DAUGHTERS OF GEORGE III by Copley

*THE AMERICAN SCHOOL by Matthew Pratt. While
Mr. West gives criticism, his students listen carefully.*

The Metropolitan Museum of Art,
Bequest of Maria De Will Jesup, 1915

THE MOUNTAIN FORD by Thomas Cole

INDEX

(Bold face indicates illustrations)